Cornish
Landscapes

JO DARKE

Cornish Landscapes

B T Batsford Ltd · London

ISBN 0 7134 4187 9

Typeset by Typewise Limited, Wembley
and printed in Hong Kong

Produced in co-operation with
Opus Books and published by
B. T. Batsford Ltd
4 Fitzhardinge Street
London W1H 0AH

CONTENTS

LIST OF ILLUSTRATIONS

Introduction

Cornwall has only one boundary and that is the south-flowing River Tamar of which the Cornish historian Charles Henderson wrote, 'So conscious was it of its destiny as a frontier that it elected to rise within four miles of Severn Sea, and thus has done its utmost to make Cornwall an island'. The would-be island is a bony promontory of water and stone which continues the thrust of England's south-west peninsula for 80 miles into the ocean, tilting along its breadth from the Atlantic heights to the soft underbelly of Cornwall's Channel shores. From this long plateau of sandstones and shales a series of granite bosses protrudes, the second-highest in England – but Cornwall's highest – being Bodmin Moor, which is divided from Devon's Dartmoor by the Tamar in its valley, and the surrounding countryside. In the north-east corner of the moor the gentle peaks of Brown Willy and Rough Tor form Cornwall's greatest heights, and from their summits on a clear day can be seen the long south-westward stretch of Cornwall's spine. The first of its granite vertebrae offers a lunar prospect of white clay cones as Hensbarrow Down, scarred but productive, sprawls above the clay ports of Par, Charlestown and Pentewan in St Austell Bay. Far beyond, on Carnmenellis Moor, Bronze-Age people once panned for tin. Further still the craggy hills of West Penwith are all but surrounded by sea, for the neck of this squarish peninsula narrows to a width of four miles between Hayle Estuary and Mount's Bay. Twenty-eight miles off Land's End the Isles of Scilly, tiny islands of rocks and flowers, are all that remain of Cornwall's tail.

Nature has been kind to Cornwall, surrounding its 226 miles of sea coast with the sheltered waters of the English Channel and the Atlantic gulf stream, giving it a moist and mild climate, watering it with long winding estuaries and lavishing foliage on its cliffs or crags. The high northern cliffs endure the Atlantic rollers which retreat on the ebb to reveal long sandy beaches or tranquil coves. The southern cliffs dip down to milder waters whose tumultuous rage can equal that of the Atlantic in times of storm. Rivers rise on the granite moorlands and stream south, flowing through deep wide *rias*, cut before the last Ice Age, which flooded when the ice sheets melted and raised the sea-level to make broad estuaries winding between fields and trees from deep inland. In the far south-west the wide crescent of Mount's Bay with its bamboo and palms and flower fields is held within England's most westerly and southerly points, the rugged moors of West Penwith and the Lizard peninsula's dark cliffs of Serpentine.

No part of Cornwall is further than 20 miles from the sea, and ancient settlers came from overseas rather than by land, although later Cornwall and Wales gave refuge to Britons fleeing from Anglo-Saxon and Danish invaders advancing from England's south-eastern shores. The Romans came, saw and traded for tin but otherwise made little impact on what was an Iron-Age culture whose people fished, farmed, quarried and mined. Celtic missionaries came from Ireland and Wales in the fifth to seventh centuries, and left their heritage of improbable Saints' names attached to churches and holy wells through the length and breadth of the land. The culture and language of these Celtic people lived on for 700 years after political and religious capitulation to the Saxons and then the Normans. Cultural integration was longest resisted and even today the old language echoes in place names and surnames while in the clayworks and quarries, in the fishing syndicates and on the farms, it is the Cornish dialect that can be heard. In Cornish homes 'proper' pasties, yeast buns, saffron cake and cream are made, and hog's pudding takes the place of supermarket sausages. You can tell a family's political affiliations if you know whether they are 'chapel' or 'church'.' One of the finest compliments you can receive in Cornwall is to be told you are 'a man to go to sea with' or, if you are not ethnic Cornish, to be treated as 'One and All'.

A road map for visitors of the early eighteenth century, in an accompanying note, explains '...the Tin of this County (for which it was famed in the days of Herodotus) is esteemed the best & finest in Europe, & is not much inferior to Silver...the Men are strong & boisterous, great Wrestlers, and Healthy. This County is enriched likewise by the great quantity of Fish especially Pilchards, which are taken on these Coasts. Its other Comodities are French & Bearded Wheat, & other Corn...' From the earliest days, Cornwall's economy and culture have been dominated by water, soil and stone and, in turn, man's response to his environment has left its imprint. From the moment you cross the Tamar, the uncompromisingly Cornish aspect of the landscape asserts itself. The wildest country is rarely bleak, for lichen covers roofs and walls, gorse blazes on cliffs or moors, and on the exposed Atlantic clifftops are stone walls topped with wind-bent, feathery tamarisk. In the south, luxuriant river valleys are likely to be spanned by mighty viaducts of granite, carrying railways.

Cornish people, like people in all English counties, take special pride in their homeland whose name comes from the Celtic *corn*, meaning 'promontory,' and the Saxon *wealas*, meaning 'strangers.' Geography and history lend strength to the notion that theirs is a land apart.

1 *Across the Tamar*

First impressions of the 'delectable Duchy' will vary according to the bridges crossed, for the Tamar commencing its southward journey from the towering Atlantic cliffs runs the gamut of the Cornish landscape. Flowing to the east of rugged Bodmin Moor, it conjoins with other rivers to meet the Hamoaze which broadens between fields and trees before greeting the English Channel in Plymouth Sound – part Devon part Cornwall, yet already characteristic of the milder South Cornish shores. The Tamar estuary is crossed by the great wrought-iron rail bridge built between Plymouth and Saltash by Brunel and opened in 1859, or by the road bridge of a century later built alongside, or by the car ferry plying the Hamoaze between Devonport and Torpoint. Further upstream the roads cross medieval granite bridges set in meadows or in

Hotels and beach huts line the harbour entrance at Bude, Cornwall's most northerly resort.

Atlantic grandeur: the north Cornish coastline viewed from Efford Beacon, looking northward past Bude toward Crooklets Beach and Morwenstow.

steep woods, and finally the main road from Barnstaple to Bude crosses the boundary over the high wedge of marshy land that welds Cornwall to Devon and to England. Here the ocean thunders against Cornish cliffs which are high and forbidding, but which blaze with gorse in summer. In the combes old villages or churches shelter among wind-pruned trees while the seaside bungalows and resorts of the present century adorn the ocean's edge, sacrificing shelter for a sea view. Bude is the most northerly resort on the Atlantic coast, and first grew as a small outport for its mother-town, Stratton. Although seaside amusements are provided, as well as Atlantic rollers pounding along the broad flat sands, it is evident that the resort developed alongside the working town. The river winding round joins a canal that was constructed in the early 1800s to carry fertilising sand to Launceston and Holsworthy in Devon, and now makes a

pleasant boating place. It is perhaps typical of the Cornishman's pragmatic outlook that during the Georgian period, when the would-be watering places of England's south coast were creating Terraces, Crescents and Esplanades, Bude was building cottages for workmen on the canal basin and the port, which still handles commercial vessels. Between the canal and the river, in the centre of town, one can play cricket or golf on the green space known as the Shalder Hills where Sir Goldsworthy Gurney, who constructed Britain's first steam carriage, built a small castellated folly called Bude Castle. The soft cliff turf of the Summerleaze Downs, above the town, makes an agreeable place for walking.

Bude's position as a resort is enhanced by the majestic views from its cliffs to south and north. From nearby Efford Beacon, 300 feet high, clear weather will show all the drama of the north coast stretching south-west to take in Widemouth Bay,

the dark heights of the Dizzard, the cliffs encompassing Crackington Haven and then Boscastle, Tintagel, and far beyond, Trevose Head. Across-country, due south on Bodmin Moor, the brooding outlines of Brown Willy and Roughtor (Row Tor) appear – at 1375 and 1311 feet, Cornwall's highest peaks. Northward are dark twisted cliffs, and the sheltered combes of Cornwall's northernmost parish Morwenstow.

The lonely church of St Morwenna stands near its holy well and its vicarage, seeming to grow out of the hillside and stunted woodlands, and within sound of the surf. Like most Cornish churches dedicated to saintly missionaries from Wales and Ireland who settled here in Cornwall's 'Golden Age', this church is isolated from later settlements in the parish. The Norman church was largely rebuilt in the fifteenth century but, uncharacteristically, much of it has survived medieval and Victorian restoration. The

beautifully carved bench ends were said to have been salved from Victorian restorers at work in nearby churches by R S Hawker, the eccentric poet-parson who served this parish from 1834-75. A compassionate and emotional man, Hawker also salved the bodies of dead seamen from the many wrecks along this treacherous coast and gave them proper burial beneath the twisted trees of his churchyard:

> They came in paths of storm – they found
> This quiet home in Christian ground.

Hawker became a legend in his own time, loved by his parishioners, remembered also today for having introduced Harvest Festival, and for his *Song of the Western Men*, better-known as *Trelawney*. The driftwood hut where he dreamed and wrote his *Quest of the Sangraal* can still be seen on the cliff. The deep valleys embedded with summer flowers and even the cruel rocks,

The gateway to Cornwall: Launceston entered by its South Gate, all that survives of the medieval walls. An art gallery, The Gallery Over the Arch, occupies the room above the gate.

11

softened by silken summer seas, must have moved him to write, 'Paradise: How lovely must its fields have been since even Earth, the land of our Exile, is so surpassingly fair.' This is a region of Cornwall whose churches are 'surpassingly fair,' many with Norman doorways and a wealth of locally carved bench-ends, some by Michael Chuke of Kilkhampton who was a pupil of Grinling Gibbons. A strongly Royalist region even for Cornwall, most churches hold the Royal Arms of Charles II, especially well carved. The woodland church at Launcells was one of the few Cornish churches that escaped over-zealous Victorian restoration, and soft Cornish light is shed through clear glass on Chuke's elaborately-carved Arms and other treasures within.

From Holsworthy near Devon's north coast Launceston traffic crosses the Tamar at Netherbridge, a granite hump-back of three arches, but the 'time-honoured threshold of Cornwall', so called by the historian Charles Henderson, was the Normans' Polston B ridge which formerly carried A30 traffic from Exeter to Launceston – Cornwall's sentinel town, and county town until 1838. From there the road crossed Bodmin Moor on its way to the far south-west. Henderson quoted a thirteenth-century Charter's title for the road as *Via Regalis Cornubiensis*, 'The Royal Cornish Way'. The medieval bridge has been superseded by the modern Dunheved Bridge further downstream and the A30, now by-passing Launceston, still carries much of Cornwall's traffic. Charles Henderson's favourite, 'the fairest bridge in the two Shires', was the medieval Greystone Bridge, which carries traffic between North Cornwall and Tavistock, on the edge of Dartmoor. From any crossing, Launceston, 'Gateway to Cornwall,' makes a handsome introduction. It is a grey hill town commanded by the ruin of its castle,

Dunheved, and steeply entered under a pointed arch which is all that remains of the old town walls. The town began on a neighbouring hill, gathered about its Celtic monastery, and its name records the Celtic and Saxon religious settlements of St Stephen. The present church of St Stephen which was built on the site of the old monastery and dedicated in 1259 remained the parish church of Launceston through the Middle Ages, and the old town gives splendid views of Launceston and its castle from the nearby hill. Launceston's present parish church of St Mary Magdalene was originally built as the Norman castle's chapel, but was reconstructed in the sixteenth century by Sir Henry Trecarrel of Lezant after the death of his infant son, and then his wife. Trecarrel discontinued building operations on his manor house and poured his wealth into this extraordinary church, every square inch of which is lovingly carved on the outside from that hardest of hard stone, granite, in friezes, symbols, beasts and tropical fruits, and in scenes from the lives of the Saints. It was not until the fifteenth century that more sophisticated instruments and techniques had made possible the widespread use of this stone in churches and manors, and these carvings are a triumph of Cornish craftsmanship.

The Launceston poet Charles Causley has written of Trecarrel's building, and also of a great stoneworker from the haunting landscape of Bodmin Moor:

Here lived Burnard who with his finger's bone
Broke syllables of light from the moorstone,
Spat on the genesis of dust and clay,
Rubbed with sure hands the blinded light of day,
And through the seasons of the talking sun
Walked, calm as God, the fields of Altarnun.

The nineteenth-century sculptor Nevil Northey

13

The gentler face of Bodmin Moor, a 12-mile square tract of predominantly rough pasture, marsh and granite.

Burnard was born in the moorland village of Altarnun, rose meteorically to become a leading sculptor of his day, and exhibited at the Royal Academy. In later years, affected by the death of his daughter, he succumbed to alcoholism and threw off his fame to tramp the roads between London and Cornwall. There in Camborne, in 1878, he was given a pauper's funeral – his pall bearers a team of stonemasons that happened to be carrying out restorations to the parish church. Burnard's relief profile of John Wesley, which he carved when he was 18, is seen over the door of Altarnun's Wesleyan meeting house, a Georgian chapel of typical nonconformist simplicity. Altarnun too is a typical moorland village, the solid cottages of 'moorstone' – local granite – sheltering in a valley of weathered trees, watered by a stream which is crossed by an old stone bridge. The church, lofty and spacious like its parish, is dedicated to the mother of St David but contains much in carvings and furnishing which is 'local' to the village and the windy moors beyond.

Altarnun is reached by The Royal Cornish Way of medieval times fairly soon after it reaches the moor from Launceston. This fast road which carries the 'summer trade' to all parts of Cornwall via Bodmin gives tantalising glimpses of the moor's moods which are best discovered on minor roads or, with care, on foot. The ancient and beautiful places around Brown Willy or Rough Tor, or the Hantergantick Gorge, are best seen at close quarters where numerous prehistoric remains people the moor, in the imagination, with herdsmen, farmers and traders, and make it far different from the lonely place it seems today. This north-western side of the moor is generally less dramatic – though no less atmospheric – than that which lies south-west of the bisecting highway. Here even bleak Dozmary Pool, passed by a turning south near Daphne du Maurier's Jamaica Inn, can look wicked at certain times and in certain weather. According to legend this sheet of water received the sword of Excalibur, and was the site of a hellish task set for the giant Tregeagle. It seems likely that it was a flint trading post in Neolithic times, unwelcoming though it appears. East of the pool lies the Fowey River, after which the moor was once named, and near the southern edge of the moor the river splashes down the Golytha Falls through light, mossy woodland of willow and oak over a granite bed. Looming east of this fairytale valley are the sprawling heights of Caradon Hill and its

disused mines that produced much of Cornwall's copper last century, at a time when the county supplied two-thirds of the world demand. Northward across the valley the moors are dark with granite boulders and abound in antiquities like the Bronze-Age stone circle called the Hurlers, frozen to stone for playing on a Sunday, or the Neolithic chambered tomb Trethevy Quoit constructed of massive moorland slabs. Just as remarkable is the Cheesewring, a granite outcrop eroded along its natural fault lines into a top-heavy stack, smoothed by wind and rain. From here the view reaches across Cornwall to Dartmoor and Exmoor beyond.

Further west along small moorland roads, set in a parish of rushing streams, bogs, hut circles and disused tin mines, the pretty church town of St Neot clusters round the pinnacled tower and powerful porch and 15 windows of medieval glass which make the pygmy-Saint Neot's church one of the glories of the moor. On the other side of the moor and of Bodmin the church and village of Blisland are counterparts to St Neot, although here the glory lies in the church's outstanding reconstruction work carried out by F C Eden between 1896 and 1930. Blisland is reached from Bodmin by taking a street which climbs steadily north of the town and quickly becomes a deep Cornish lane overhung with blackthorn. Although Bodmin is the Assize town and was the ecclesiastical centre of Cornwall from St Petroc's arrival in the sixth century throughout the Middle Ages, a rugged spirit characterised its people. In the twelfth century, French Canons visiting the town were set upon for scorning the assertion that King Arthur lived. Within a single century Bodmin men led the disastrous 1497 revolt against excessive taxation, supported the Pretender Perkin Warbeck, and organised the Prayer Book Rebellion, for which its mayor was hanged. In St Petroc's Church Prior Vyvyan's tomb carved of catacleuse slate and the remarkable Norman font, and the twelfth-century casket that once held St Petroc's bones, make worthy reminders of this moorland town's more tranquil past – all hidden from the grey, busy streets of today's social and market centre.

The Tamar itself creates some of Cornwall's loveliest landscape, particularly around Gunnislake Bridge, set deep in a wooded valley, which was built of granite early in the sixteenth century by Sir Piers Edgecumbe of Cotehele House. Although Cotehele is one of England's finest and most complete examples of a medieval manor house, its granite buildings grouped about their courtyards in gardens of native and sub-tropical plants make it intrinsically Cornish. The house was rebuilt by the Edgecumbes between the fifteenth and sixteenth centuries and then abandoned by the family later in the 1500s for a grander residence at Mount Edgecumbe. It has remained almost untouched since, and was handed to the National Trust by the same family with the armour, furnishings and huge tapestries that have adorned it since the sixteenth and seventeenth centuries. This was the romantic setting for the escape of Sir Richard Edgecumbe from the Earl of Bodrugan, an assassin employed by Richard III. Richard Carew's *Survey of Cornwall*, published in 1602, gives a dramatic account:

...he was hotly pursued and narrowly searched for. Which extremity taught him a sudden policy, to put a stone in his cap and tumble the same into the water while these rangers were fast at his heels, who looked down after the noise and seeing the cap swimming thereon, supposed that he had desperately drowned himself, gave over their further hunting, and left him liberty to shift away and ship over into Brittany...

The Carew family lived nearby at Antony, above the Lynher Estuary, for 500 years, and their Classic mansion is now open to the public through the National Trust. The nearby Mount Edgecumbe was said to have been earmarked by the Duke of Medina Sidonia, Commander of the Armada, as his own reward in the event of England's defeat. The lush and woody south Cornish shores, whose gentle headlands can be seen in a sequence of decreasing shadowy shapes from Rame to the Lizard, must have been a fair prospect in the eyes of the invaders – as they are for visitors today.

Trethevy Quoit, a Neolithic chamber tomb on Bodmin Moor's Caradon Hill, north-west of St Cleer.

2 The Riviera Coast

In his guidebook to the Cornish Riviera of 1911 Sydney Heath wrote,

...the delectable Duchy was a singularly isolated strip of land until the magic connecting link was forged by Brunel. Indeed it is not too much to say that Cornwall owes its present favourable position as a health resort almost entirely to the genius of Brunel and the enterprise of the Great Western Railway.

The first stop after Saltash in Brunel's 'magic connecting link' is St Germans, the old unspoiled village climbing up from the head of the River Lynher to its cathedral-like Norman church. Its predecessor was the premier church in Cornwall during the Saxons' brief rule but it fell victim to the long process of uniting the Cornish culture with the English. Centuries later, in forging the 'connecting link,' Brunel and the GWR accelerated the intermingling of cultures, for the trains and then the family cars opened up Cornwall at a time when traditional industries were on the decline. Old ports whose smuggling days were over and whose fishing or tin exporting were reduced colour-washed their cottages, and abandoned themselves to tourism. In places the original industries continued alongside, some on a small scale and some flourishing like the St Austell clay industry. This has created a further duality in the changing Cornish landscape, nowhere more marked than on South Cornwall's scenic and industrious coast, the destination of the Cornish Riviera Express.

Beautiful Looe is the first popular holiday spot along the Riviera coast. It retains an active fishing fleet, is famous for shark fishing, and has long since made a car park of the old Copper Ore Quay, once the outlet for the rich mining and quarrying areas around Caradon Hill. One of Britain's loveliest rail lines, the Looe-Liskeard railway carried the ore through the East Looe valley from Liskeard, a town of slate-hung lanes and handsome terraces. The East Looe is the greater of two rivers, both beautiful in their glens, that stream down from beneath the moor and meet to issue beneath the Victorian bridge which unites East Looe with West Looe. On this cliff-sheltered site the town grew prosperous by fishing, augmented at varying periods by smuggling, or exporting stone and metal, and recently by tourism. East Looe's sixteenth-century Guildhall today houses a local history museum, and at the working harbour or in the narrow winding streets there still lives an atmosphere of earlier days. In West Looe the Chapel of St Nicholas was used as a guildhall in Elizabethan times and then a school until the mid-nineteenth century, when it was returned to sacred use and its interior restored, using timbers, it is said, from the Spanish ship *San Josef* which was captured by Lord Nelson. One Cornish mile off Hannafore Cliff looms Looe Island, open in season for visits by the small boats which give summer sport to the visitors and year-round livelihood to the fishermen.

Even more picturesque, and possibly more crowded in summer despite a ban on cars in its precipitous streets, is the fishing village of Polperro. The village has grown below the meeting of two streams which rush together down a cleft in the cliffs between the cottages slanting to the harbour where fishing boats shelter. In summer the Mesembryanthemum covering the rocky slopes and the ranks of white or pastel cottages give Polperro a Mediterranean look but on winter days when huge waves lick at the harbour walls one can see Polperro for what it has always been – a stone fishing village, dependent for its survival on the weather. Fishing

and smuggling were Polperro's livelihoods, and in the eighteenth century every cottage had its hide. Among the oldest is the leaning Elizabethan cottage where Sir Arthur Quiller-Couch's grandfather, Jonathan Couch, practised as the village doctor and won fame as a writer and naturalist. The hilly country between the Looe and Fowey estuaries, with Polperro a third of the way along, slopes to a coast of high and pleasant cliffs where footpaths plunge through bracken to secret coves. West of Pencarrow Head Lantic Bay curves round, and the parish church of Lanteglos nestles on an inland slope by a farm, lonely in the centre of its parish. A woody valley follows from

here to Pont at the head of Pont Pill, one of the Fowey River's magic creeks.

A ruined fort guards each bank at the mouth of the river, by Polruan on the east and Fowey across the water. Five miles up-river at the head of still-navigable waters stands Lostwithiel, a stannary town and capital of Cornwall in ancient times. The peaceful, secret river broadens deep inland between woods and fields, entered by other rivers, with churches and villages overlooking the water or standing at its edge. To the west, Golant, Lantyan, and above them Castle Dore have strong claims as the setting for the romance of King Mark, Ysolde, and Tristan. On the other

St Germans, in past centuries the most important church in Cornwall, viewed from the beautiful formal gardens of Port Eliot.

side of the river, at the head of its own creek, Lerryn is as much visited by river as by road. The remains of an ancient earthwork, the Giant's Hedge, can be made out in places as it rolls across-country toward Lanreath:

The Devil one day, having nothing to do
Built a great hedge from Lerryn to Looe.

Further up-river the church of St Winnow stands by the water, its churchyard projecting on a spit of land with a landing stage for the congregation.

Lostwithiel at the navigable head of the river has a medieval grid of narrow streets, mercifully by-passed and overlooked. Along the riverside granite wharves recall the town's hectic days when tinners brought their ore for assaying and taxing to the stannary court and treasury offices, whose buildings survive from 1280 in Quay Street. Spanning the river from Quay Street is Lostwithiel's graceful bridge with five arches, thought to date from 1437. Just as graceful as the bridge is the fourteenth-century church of St Bartholomew, its clerestory and windows and octagonal spire bearing traces of French influence like many of the buildings around. During the Civil War, the church survived without serious injury – unlike the Norman castle Restormel occupying the tall shoulder of a hill rising out of woods and farmlands a mile upstream, stormed by Sir Richard Grenville for the King to the detriment of its thirteenth-century walls. Today this fine medieval castle on its domed hill is cared for so tidily by the Department of the Environment that the words of John Norden seem somehow out of place even though no structural alterations have been made since he wrote, in the late sixteenth century.

The whole castle beginneth to mourne, and to wringe out harde stones for tears, that she was imbraced, visited and delighted with greate princes, is now desolate, forsaken and forlorne; the cannon needes not batter, nor the pioner to undermine, nor powder to blow up this so famous a pyle, for time and tirranie hath wrought her desolation.

The hidden places on the Fowey River must look the same today as they did in the roistering days when Fowey was Cock of the Channel and the Fowey Gallants snubbed even the great Cinque Ports, and continued their own war with France after England's was formally over. Edward IV, his patience at an end, sent a messenger demanding an end to this behaviour. The messenger returned with a severed ear, whereupon Edward enlisted the help of Dartmouth in breaking and dismantling the great chain that could be stretched from fort to fort across Fowey's harbour mouth to prevent unwanted entry. The rebel captains were hanged at Lostwithiel and the ships were confiscated from the town that had sent more fighters to Calais than any other English Channel port. Despite this serious set-back, the port has always enjoyed prominence in this coast's defence and trade. Overlooking this harbour, high in the town, is Fowey's fourteenth-century church with its great carved tower of Pentewan stone, one of the tallest in Cornwall. Rising above the church is Fowey's pride, Place House, rebuilt by the Treffrys after the French raid of 1434 when Lady Treffry successfully defended the original house, and in doing so protected the townsfolk who had taken refuge inside. Since then Place has been much altered, notably in the nineteenth century when it was almost entirely rebuilt by Joseph Treffry, with immense charm. Both Place and the church seem to grow out of the folds of Fowey's hilly streets, and from high above the town you get tantalising glimpses of water and fields beyond. Early this century Sir Arthur Quiller-Couch, looking down from his window, described Fowey harbour: '...vessels of every nation and men of large experience are forever coming and going...'. Today's harbour holds moorings for sailing dinghies and holiday cruisers, while the 10,000-ton clay boats plough through on their way up to the deep-water docks. The late Claude Berry, author and journalist, was a Padstow man but still he could write, 'the rhythm of Fowey's life is essentially Cornish. In her streets and along her waterside I hear the steady, comforting beat of Cornwall's heart'.

The lifeblood is the china clay that is quarried from the Hensbarrow Downs behind St Austell Bay where 'The pyramids rise pure in colour and line' around the sprawling moors. A L Rowse was born within sight of Carclaze, one of Cornwall's first clay works and once the world's largest tin mine, situated on the edge of the clay industry's commercial centre, St Austell. This is a sober granite town situated on a slope about a mile from St Austell Bay, the clayworked moor at its head and the brilliant sea at its feet, and dark firs or palms in the gardens here and there. On the east of St Austell Bay, as described in A L Rowse's poem *The Road to Roche*,

...the Gribbin
Pushes a long lizard paw into the sea,

topped by its red-and-white striped Daymark. On

East Looe, and the Victorian bridge which links it with West Looe. The towns were amalgamated in 1883.

Overleaf Polperro Harbour. One of the southern coast's most popular beauty spots, Polperro's old buildings and narrow streets retain the character of a Cornish fishing town.

the west, the land juts southward at Black Head. Among the small havens and the bays between, Par and Charlestown are busy processing and exporting clay. Charlestown was built by Charles Rashleigh especially to handle the newly-discovered material that was eventually to take over where tin and copper left off, making Cornwall one of the world's largest producers of kaolin. The whole place can be seen in a *coup d'oeil* from the cliffs to Porthpean: the colour-washed Georgian terrace perching above the deep granite cut where the clay boats slide in to be loaded two at a time, the grassy slope below the terrace, the pier where people fish and walk on Sundays. This small port trades in animal feed fertilizer and equipment for water-skiing and skin diving, popular sports on this Riviera Coast.

China clay, the product of decomposing granite, was first discovered in Britain on Tregonning Hill near Mount's Bay by William Cookworthy in the mid-eighteenth century, and soon afterwards greater quantities were found around St Austell. The cones or long rectangular hills are of gritty quartz sand, a waste product separated from the powdery clay, and they make the moors look unearthly but not unsightly. Even so the blind poet Jack Clemo has described his birthplace in the clay country as a 'broken, scarred and unkempt land'. Clemo's eloquent description, sadly, could be applied to much of Cornwall's most startlingly beautiful coastal scenery, ruined beyond redemption by indifferently designed buildings constructed from cheap materials, and producing for the county little more benefit than a sea view for their summer season occupants. A favoured picnic place for those who live on these productive moors is Roche Rock which looms up from the northern edge of the clay country, a jagged outcrop of schorl surmounted by a fifteenth-century chapel and a hermit's cell, refuge of the giant Tregeagle who played chess with the hermit by standing in the bracken and leaning through the chapel window which we can reach by means of a winding and tortuous stairway cut into the rock. A beautiful local picnic spot is Luxulyan Valley, which runs inland from St Blazey and is crossed by Treffry's granite viaduct striding mightily through the lush green of Luxulyan's trees and ferns. Just west of St Austell is another 'White River,' an ancient tin-streaming river the Winnick, which enters the sea at Pentewan Beach. The village and Joseph Treffry's harbour lie at the bottom of a perilous hill, and from the

town square stone houses in burgeoning gardens climb up to a small Regency terrace with Classic church; further along toward the sea is the chapel. By contrast, Mevagissey has a Mediterranean touch and is very much a fishing town, slatey and steep, and busy too with shark fishing or pleasure trips which have taken the place of last century's pilchard seining and boat building, when the town also specialised in fast sailing boats designed for smuggling. Past picturesque Portmellon, still a boat-building village, the cliffs reach south to Chapel Point and the 100-foot drop where in Charles Causley's poetic account,

> …at Bodrugan's Leap the deep
> still wrings its watery hands…

Here the Earl of Bodrugan is said to have escaped daringly from the vengeful Edgecumbes, although Causley's poem gives a more sombre ending.

From Chapel Point past Gorran Haven and beautiful Vault Beach the Dodman rears southward into the Channel, brilliant in summer with heather and gorse, the seas around it perilous in storms. An Iron-Age hill fort occupies Dodman Point, and from this ancient look-out the view sweeps all along the romantic and often-treacherous coast to Rame Head, and westward past Falmouth's Carrick Roads to the Lizard. Until the Roseland peninsula is reached just west of Nare Head, no major or secondary road comes close to these shores edged with plump farmland. A road and a river wind through to Porthluney Cove past Caerhays Castle, built by Nash in 1808, with its backdrop of towering Magnolia trees, Rhododendrons, beech and pine. Minor roads link Portholland, Portloe and Veryan, or rough coastal paths lead across the cliffs and dip down to unpeopled coves. Portloe's fishing village nestles around its harbour, flanked by cliffs, and a steep climb out of the village leads to gentle Nare Head and Gerrans Bay where the coast can be seen ranging southward toward Zone Point. Inland, deep lanes lead to Veryan which attracts many visitors because of its thatched cottages and mysterious round houses, each topped by a cross, and its church set amid sub-tropical plants. Some miles northward, the River Fal flows in from the moors past Tregony and its estuary winds out into the broad waters known as the Carrick Roads, part of the river system of the Fal, the most magic and complex of south Cornwall's waterways. Between the Fal and the long southward stretch of coast from Nare to

Restormel Castle, north-west of Lostwithiel, the medieval capital of Cornwall.

25

Perhaps the clay spoil-heaps behind St Austell mar the landscape, but the pale conical forms, and the turquoise water of the claypits, can give a beautiful and unearthly appearance.

Zone is Roseland peninsula, as lovely as its name

The peninsula, thrusting southward, is pierced by the Percuil River and its tributaries, and the traveller encounters a confusion of views. Rivers wind between woods and fields; sea spray breaks against black rocks, and the distant cliffs of the Lizard can be seen; the castles of St Mawes and Pendennis guard the mouth of Carrick Roads where cargo boats and pleasure boats and the white sails of oyster dredgers speck waters that are enfolded in the Cornish countryside. The National Trust owns Anthony Head and its small lighthouse near the southern tip of the peninsula, with some pleasant beaches and cliff walks, and countryside including pine woods and an old tide mill. Near here is St Anthony-in-Roseland, where the church and a Victorian Tudor-style mansion, now a hotel, face the yachtsman's paradise St Mawes across Percuil River. The mansion, known as Place, incorporates part of an old priory and can be entered from the church with its octagonal, slate-hung spire. Across the river on the way south to St Mawes, a turning to the right dives down to the town's mother-church, St Just-in-Roseland. This well-loved place

stands by the waters of a small creek and is entered through a lych-gate from which a path plunges between tombstones and flowering shrubs. The lych-gate giving entry from the valley has a granite cattle grid, while the upper lych-gate stands higher than the church's fifteenth-century tower and the surrounding trees, through which the glint of water can be seen.

The road to St Mawes travels high along the spine of its peninsula, giving splendid views before descending between narrow streets to the quay. This has long been a centre for the yachting fraternity, and its marine villas and waterfront hotels give it an affluent feel that does nothing to disturb its charm. In the Civil War the clover-leaf castle built by Henry VIII south-west of the town capitulated immediately while Pendennis across Carrick Roads held out for five months under siege. Of the two Carew explains, 'St Mawes lieth lower and better to annoy shipping, but

Roche Rock; granite on granite. The ruin of a hermit's chapel and the surrounding boulder-strewn terrain make this a popular spot for local outings.

Pendennis standeth higher and stronger to defend itself.' The broad sheet of water known as the Carrick Roads, so-called because it could accommodate the medieval carracks – great merchantmen from the Mediterranean – is entered at the mouth by estuaries from the east and west, the Percuil and Penryn, and by other minor creeks as it stretches northward through rural Cornwall. At the King Harry Ferry the water narrows, but higher up is joined by the rivers Fal, Tresillian, Allen and Kenwyn. Tranquil and mysterious in the sleepy air these radiating rivers broaden from deep inland, piercing the fat farmlands with treeshaded creeks. At the head of this system, and at the confluence of the Allen and the Kenwyn, is Truro, Cornwall's city, its cathedral proudly placed at its ancient heart.

Truro was a medieval stannary town, but its later wealth came from the mining boom of the eighteenth and nineteenth centuries, when the river which has since silted with mine refuse delivered timbers from Scandinavia among other things for use as props in deep mine workings, and exported the tin and copper ores. In the eighteenth century Truro was the fashionable centre of Cornwall, and the centre of high life was its Assembly Rooms whose facade still stands at the cathedral's west end. Truro's Georgian streets, granite Lemon Street or Walsingham Terrace, recall those pace-setting days. The cathedral is only 100 years old but incorporates the south aisle of the fifteenth-century parish church. Massive and graceful, it gathers the old streets of the city around its towers and spires. Inside, the granite of the original church echoed by use of granite in parts of the new makes a contrast with arches and columns of creamy Bath stone. This was the first cathedral to be built in England since Wren's St Paul's, and it is seen as a particularly fine and sensitive example of Victorian architecture. Truro is one of Cornwall's most elegant towns, and well-suited to its present rôle as the county's administrative centre. Its museum, the finest in Cornwall, has excellent displays of local culture and natural history, as well as the celebrated Rashleigh collection of minerals from Cornish mines. Nevil Northey Burnard's marble bust of Richard Trevithick is displayed, and paintings by Opie hang in the art gallery. Kneller's portrait of the Cornish 'giant' Antony Payne hangs half-way up the main staircase. Born at Stratton, Payne served as Sir Bevil Grenville's retainer against the Parliamentarians and established order 'by the mere terror of his presence and strength,' R S Hawker tells us in an essay. The portrait depicts an immense, but gentle, man.

Just as the long estuaries of the Looe, Fowey and Fal divide and cut off the coastal lands, so the Fal's tributaries, splayed like the veins of a leaf, isolate small segments of rural countryside. Lanes wriggle between woods, marshes and farms to end at villages or manors, or at the water's edge. The Tresillian River slides past the tree-shaded villages of St Clements and Malpas – 'bad passage' in French – as it broadens towards the Truro River. This ancient ferry gave access across the Tresillian River to Truro from the village of St Michael Penkivel, which belongs to the estate of Tregothnan. The battlemented mansion house is the seat of the Boscawens, Earls of Falmouth, and was built in the style of a Tudor castle by William Wilkins early in the 1800s. With its deer park, woodlands, avenues and lawns, it is guardian of the lands held between the Truro River and the Fal. Down-river is another ancient ferry, the King Harry, which carries motor traffic to the west bank of the Fal close to the sub-tropical grounds of Trelissick. This mansion was restyled in the 1820s to emerge with a grand porticoed entrance and echoes of a Grecian temple, and a luxuriant array of shrubs and trees. Below Trelissick, which is in the keeping of the National Trust, the waters widen and beome busy with yachts and pleasure boats, or sailing boats dredging oyster beds. Feock at the turn of the creek is an old village given to holiday villas, and one can sail up here to the head of the creek where Perranworthal and the small town of Devoran seem unchanged since they became industrialised at the end of the eighteenth century, except that the warehouses and old factories occupying the waters' edge have been abandoned, while the Georgian cottages are still occupied. These towns stand on the Truro-Falmouth road just before it swings south toward Penryn which was a significant river port when the usurper Falmouth comprised no more than a couple of hamlets too close for comfort to the Channel waters. Penryn's old granite houses, sloping cottage gardens, town hall and town square are given a sense of purpose and continuity by a flourishing granite-processing industry. Facing the wooded farmland on the east banks of the Carrick Roads, on the squarish peninsula made by the Penryn estuary and Mylor Creek just below Restronguet, are the popular villages of Mylor and Flushing. The waterside church of St Melorus incorporates Caen stone which could be delivered by boat to

Mevagissey, fishing town and tourist haven on Cornwall's south coast. The present name can be traced to the town's patron saints Meva and Issey, or Ida.

the site, but much older is Cornwall's tallest Celtic cross, now placed outside the south door. Across the peninsula on the Falmouth edge of the Penryn River, the Flemish-style cottages of Flushing are said to have been built for Dutch engineers who came over to build Falmouth Harbour for the Killigrews. They would be rewarded today to find it Cornwall's largest port.

Falmouth's siting and climate would be ideal for any one of its rôles as sea port, fishing town, holiday and yachting resort. It presents its working face to the sheltered north, looking across the Penryn estuary, while its villas and hotels of the railway age face the sea. Before Henry VIII had built his castles at the mouth of Falmouth estuary, inland towns like Penryn and Truro were the river's main ports. When Sir Walter Raleigh, returning from his trip to Guinea, noted the potential of Falmouth's present site, it was occupied by a mansion belonging to the piratical Killigrews. They developed town and port in the seventeenth century and prosperity grew with the era of the Falmouth Packet when the port handled the Royal Mail from overseas between 1688 and 1852. The railways saved Falmouth, for they brought holidaymakers and reinforced the usefulness of Falmouth's docks when the mail packet trade was removed to Southampton and Liverpool and when the town's other industry, the pilchard fisheries, was running down. The town still thrives as a port while the harbour and its creeks are ideal for yachtsmen, and the palms, beaches and languid air make this a relaxing spot for those whose holidays turn them to idleness. Another Cornwall lies to the far south-west.

Subtropical plants and spreading lawns characterise the gardens of Trelissick, 5 miles south of Truro on the Fal.

Opposite St Mawes Castle, built in the form of a clover leaf as part of Henry VIII's coastal defence system

3 The Far South-West

Penetrating westward to form the top edge of the Lizard peninsula, the Helford Passage is as remote and secret as any of the south coast *rias*. It shelters exquisite river villages like Helford, or Durgan; exotic gardens, the sloping vistas of Glendurgan; tree-canopied *pills*, notably Frenchman's Creek of Daphne du Maurier's popular romance; oyster beds at Port Navas and a seal sanctuary at Gweek; granite quarries at Constantine, situated at the head of an estuary winding in from the moors where the granite pervades. But Helford marks the end of the long Channel shoreline which looks across at France, for it is here that the rocky southern wing of Cornwall, the Lizard peninsula, protrudes to face thousands of miles of ocean and the Americas on the other side. The Lizard, and Cornwall's westward wing the Penwith peninsula, holding the curve of Mount's Bay, seem the most remote and the most unfamiliar parts of all this far-off land. Place names no longer have a foreign echo, they *are* foreign: Pedn Boar and Carrick Luz, Gue Graze, Men-tu-Huel. The bony interior of Cornwall obtrudes instead of brooding from afar, for these wings are the last in a series of eruptive plateaux that form Cornwall's spine – Penwith, conforming, composed of granite; the Lizard a complex and unique amalgam of metamorphic rock. The Lizard air is still languid: a fig tree grows from the south wall of Manaccan Church, and almost tops its tower: but at St Keverne's Church a picture of St Christopher is prominent, while the chancel window forms a memorial to over 100 sailors drowned in 1898 when the *Mohegan* went down off the Manacle Rocks on a clear and placid evening. This is the largest of many memorials to drowned seamen in the church, whose tower and spire serve as a landmark and look across at the Manacles which stand three miles north-east off Coverack and form one of the most dreaded regions of Britain's seas. In the days of sail, a captain miscalculating and coming too close would cover over the name of his vessel to prevent detection by the ship's owner, so the story goes. The coast is less hospitable than most, with stony coves, which means that fishing villages like Cadgwith and Coverack with their thatched cottages have resisted too much development although they are much-visited, while the peculiar beauties of the inland plateau and surrounding cliffs make the Lizard especially rewarding for botanists and geologists.

The Lizard plateau has been uniformly planed by an ancient inundation of the land, but it was not high enough to develop an ice cap during the Ice Age and so formed a *refugium* where some plants escaped glaciation. Its unusual rock formation, flat and extremely hard, has a basic soil derived from shell-sand blown inland by gales, and it supports many rarities for which this is the main Cornish or British site – the best known being the handsome Cornish heath, *Erica vagans*, found on the Goonhilly Downs. Scenically the Downs are desolate and mysterious, and the huge saucer-like aerials of the GPO's Earth Station seem unearthly rather than intrusive. One of the most popular, still-beautiful places around the Lizard Point is the tiny harbour of Mullion Cove, situated at the southern end of Mount's Bay, which once with Coverack was the main smuggling base along the coast. The National Trust maintains the cove and the toy-like harbour wall, which is constructed from the hard greenstone of which the cove is formed. Further along in the same ownership is

the botanist's paradise Predannack, described in the Trust's *Guide* as a '600-acre wilderness of heath, bog, rock and stream sweeping down to the cliffs and coves below.' Kynance Cove lies between here and the Point, a marvel of many-coloured cliffs, all dark marbly serpentine, and of sands and looming caverns with rather prosaic names like the Kitchen and the Parlour and the Ladies' Bathing Pool – and, less ordinary, the Devil's Throat and the Devil's Frying Pan. This is to be seen round the Lizard Point, in the cliffs above Cadgwith. Raven's Hugo and Dolor Hugo, nearby, are caves *(fogues)* that can only be visited by boat; further north near Coverack are the rich serpentine coves of Pedn Boar, and Carrick Luz.

Serpentine is tough but workable and in Lizard Town is 'made into oddments,' but the stone has also been used locally in buildings. Landewednack Church, the most southerly in England, has a modern pulpit of serpentine, and a fine tower chequered with serpentine and granite can be seen through tall trees. Above the church the main road leads through the unlovely Lizard Town to the black cliffs and cascading cliff plants of Lizard Point, with the sea restless among the offshore reefs and the handsome buildings of the 'Lezzard Light' gleaming between Bumble Rock and the Point. Lighthouse and buildings were started in 1752 on the site of an earlier lighthouse completed in 1619 by Sir John Killigrew, developer of Falmouth. The locals, wrote Killigrew, 'affirme I take away God's grace

Mullion Cove in high summer. Storms do much damage to the quays of this picturesque miniature harbour.

from them. Their English meaning is that now they shall receive no more benefitt by shipwreck, for this will prevent yt. They have been so long used to repe profitt by the calamyties of the ruin of shipping that they clayme it heredytarye, and heavely complayne on me.' The landowning families all had wrecking rights along stretches of coast, although often this was not enough to prevent the washed up cargoes from falling into the hands of the impoverished country people. The area has its tales of shipwrecks and rich cargoes, and stories persist of bullion cast up from wrecks being buried in the sand banks near Gunwalloe Church, which itself seems to be buried in a rocky sandhill outcropping between the sea and the reedy valley beyond. All of this pleasant cove with its golf course and towans belongs to the National Trust which also owns land around Poldhu where in December 1901 Marconi sent the first transatlantic wireless message to Newfoundland.

The gateway to the Lizard is Helston, home of Henry Trengrouse whose rocket-firing apparatus for ships foundering at sea was responsible for saving more than 10,000 lives between 1870 and 1920. Helston had been a busy port in the Middle Ages but the navigable waters of the river Cober failed after the formation of the Loe Bar which closed the mouth of the river, forming the Loe Pool. Today it has an important cattle market, while the naval air station Culdrose is situated immediately to the south. It is a steep moorland town retaining the character of a Cornish stannary, even though its buildings from that period have vanished. At the top of the curving main street, Coinagehall Street, is an impressive Victorian town hall, and at the bottom of the street is a bowling green which in medieval times was the site of a fortified manor. The hilly streets make a fine background to the annual Maytime Furry celebrations – the church bells, Mayor and Corporation, top hats, flowery dresses, brass band. The Furry's origins are uncertain, but one theory has it that they represent the second feast of St Michael after Michaelmas, and this would be appropriate in a town whose church is dedicated to the Archangel Michael. The church, much restored, was rebuilt by Lord Godolphin early in the eighteenth century after the original was damaged in a storm. It still retains a spacious Georgian atmosphere which gives no hint of the town's heavy involvement in the Prayer Book Rebellion of 1549. At this time English was not understood in the remoter parts of Cornwall, and

many services were given part in Latin, part Cornish. It is said that the failure of the protest and the imposition of the English service hastened the demise of the Cornish language. A plaque at the lych-gate of St Keverne Church commemorates the local blacksmith, Mighal an Gof (Michael Joseph), who with the Bodmin lawyer Thomas Flamank led the rebellion of 1497. The people of these parts seem to have been a quarrelsome lot. The local nobility was the Godolphin family whose title derived from Sidney, the respected first Earl of Godolphin, Lord Treasurer and First Minister for Queen Anne until they quarrelled in 1710, and he was dismissed. Godolphin Hall stands facing the source of the Godolphins' wealth, the tin-rich moors; the coast, the long stretch of Mount's Bay, lies several miles to its south. Closer to the sea are the ancient tinning villages Germoe and Breage, which today are peaceful places bypassed by traffic thundering along the Helston-Marazion road, but which formerly inspired the lines,

God keep us from rocks and shelving sands
And save us from Breage and Germoe men's hands.

Breage's dominating granite church of the fifteenth century, dedicated to the Irish St Breaca, contains some remarkable medieval wall paintings, and the tombs of the Godolphins lie in the family chapel. Closer to Marazion is the pretty hamlet of Germoe whose small church sits quietly beside its stream. These old churches, peaceful now, must have seen all the harsh living, violence and heroism of the mining and 'wrecking' days. Quite close to Germoe is Cudden Point, and to the east lies Prussia Cove where John Carter ran his inn, the King of Prussia, as flimsy cover for his more profitable activities as a 'free trader'. Respected by even the revenue men for his honesty and for the discipline he imposed on his accomplices, Carter and his smuggling exploits were overlooked until he had the temerity to fire on one of the revenue sloops from his inn which was stormed and taken in retaliation.

From Tregonning Hill and Godolphin Hill, and all the heights around Mount's Bay – some bearing Neolithic remains, some cropped with early flowers, some terraced with Victorian residences, or the streets of a granite town – can be viewed the everchanging moods of St Michael's Mount. The Great Western Railway long ago laid claim to the front row of this amphitheatre's stalls by running the Cornish

Helston Furry: the townsfolk follow the Mayor and Corporation and the brass band as they weave through the streets of this ancient stannary town on Furry Day, 8 May.

St Michael's Mount with its harbour, cottages and castle is an island until low tide, when it can be reached by a causeway.

St Mary's is the largest of the Isles of Scilly's five inhabited islands, and is linked to the mainland by a regular helicopter and ferry service.

Riviera Express along the stony shore between Marazion and Penzance, between the pretty, wooded meadows and the sea with its jewel of an island. Since then, other development has made this piece of fairytale landscape into a sadly dreary stretch, but the Mount still looks exquisite and serene. The romance is maintained by the tiny harbour, steep cultivated slopes and the castle's varying architectural styles, charming interior and sweeping sea views. Formed of granite and greenstone, the Mount has always been a mysterious and venerable place. It features in legends of giants and magicians, it was visited by the Archangel Michael, it was occupied by the Celtic saints Keyne and Cadoc, and was long the site of a Celtic monastery. It passed between various noble families until in 1660 it was bought by the St Aubyn family, who still occupy the castle, and in 1954 Lord St Levan gave the Mount to the National Trust. The modern

tourist like the medieval pilgrim must approach by a half-mile-long causeway from the steep town of Marazion or, at high and half-tides, by ferry. Cobbles, rough steps, rocky ledges and more evenly cut steps lead by stages to the castle and church in their sub-tropical gardens whose elegance and style are a long way in time and culture from the days of giants, saints and monks.

The Riviera Express terminates at Penzance station, handsome in white granite and with an iron and glass roof. Penzance, too, is handsome, with its commercial area centred around Market Jew Street sloping from the direction of Marazion – once also known as Market Jew. At the top, the street divides around a fine Market House of 1836 in front of which the white marble figure of Sir Humphry Davy, inventor of the miners' lamp, looks back down the hill between the Georgian and Victorian facades of shops lining broad, elevated pavements reached by stone stairs. Most

March on St Martin's: drystone walls, tall windbreaks of Pittosporum, small narrow fields full of Cheerfulness, and the ever-present sea.

of Penzance dates from these periods, including the Egyptian House of 1830 in Chapel Street, although the former fishing town had an exciting history of Spanish raiders, Civil War and smuggling before its present development began. Penzance became Cornwall's first seaside resort and it is still the only one to boast a promenade, a dramatic place in gales when everything – sea, sky, terraces and palms – is battleship grey but for the white spray exploding over the railings onto the slithery paving stones. As if in compensation, the surrounding slopes grow early spring flowers to catch the early London market.

The flower-growing Isles of Scilly are linked to Penzance on the mainland by the *Scillonian* and the *Queen of the Isles*, or by British Airways' daily helicopter run – which perhaps will be seen to have done for the Scillies what Brunel and the GWR did for Cornwall late last century. The legendary long-lost land of Lyonesse was said to have reached from the Land's End to the Isles of Scilly, and indeed the waters, both around the Isles and between them and the mainland, are not deep. Neither are the islands high, for the loftiest point at Telegraph on St Mary's reaches 165 feet, and it is possible to imagine a period within mankind's memory when the waters were lower, and a low-lying land made Cornwall and Scilly one. Today this galaxy of islands contains all the elements that define Cornwall as a place apart yet it possesses a striking quality of its own. As in Cornwall, the contrast comes in the proportions of the elements. South Cornwall's impression is of abundant vegetation penetrated by water and punctuated with stone boulders, chapels, piers; while at the Lizard it is the stone that dominates, with the spread of bright rock-plants over the dark cliff face above restless waters. In Scilly the water and reflected sky are

Mousehole, a sturdy fishing village. The church holds an eighteenth century epitaph in Cornish and a monument to Dolly Pentreath, who claimed to be the last native Cornish speaker.

overwhelming, while the rocky outcrops all around glisten with spray, and echo with the wail of seabirds. The arbours of pines or palms, the patchwork miniature fields on south-facing slopes and the moorland crags on the northern faces, with slopes of gorse or bracken above crescents of white sand – all are subject to the humours of the sea and wind.

The largest and most important island is St Mary's, surrounded in a half-circle from north-east to south-west by the 'off-islands' St Martins, Tresco, Bryher, St Agnes and Gugh (pronounced Hugh). The archipelago lies 28 miles south-west off Land's End and 40 miles from Penzance, where flowers and tourists arrive and depart from Scilly's town, Hugh Town on St Mary's, and whence the islanders get their regular supplies of 'beef and bread'. All of these windswept islands, surrounded by numerous uninhabited islands, islets and bare rocks, are busy from November to March with the flower trade. In the chequerboard of tiny fields bordered with tall windbreaks of Fuchsia and Pittosporum, or granite drystone walls, the harsh task of planting and tending is carried out by the menfolk, who later do most of the picking, while grading and packing occupy womenfolk in the flowersheds and even the kitchens. Beginning in January with the Soleil D'Or, the daffodils and narcissi dominate the crop until April, when irises and tulips complete the season, and mundane but profitable early potatoes follow. Easter honeymooners begin the tourist flow which, as in Cornwall, has rapidly assumed prime importance. There is no sub-urban promenade on these islands; only the exotics planted in Tresco Gardens mark man's pursuit of leisure, for these are places to enjoy the birds, the plants and the elements. Wind and sea can be as cruel here as anywhere, as Scilly's history of shipwreck testifies, but on a bright

March day the clarity of the air, the vivid blue of the sea, the white sand and black rocks and brilliant magenta of Mesembryanthemum can make this journey across the lost land of Lyonesse an unforgettable one.

Apart from being the foremost mainland link with the Isles of Scilly, Penzance is the main town of the West Penwith peninsula – Cornwall's western wing and the end of her granite spine. Like Cornwall itself Penwith comes close to being an island, for the curving northern edge of the wing is nipped in at St Ives Bay, where the broad estuary of the Hayle River penetrates to within less than four miles of Mount's Bay as the crow flies. The coast to the south and west of Penzance is still dominated by Mount's Bay, in the shelter of which lie the fishing communities Newlyn and Mousehole. Both towns suffered under the Spaniards at the same time as Penzance, when they were all simple fishing

towns, and it is interesting to see how differently each has grown. At the beginning of this century Newlyn was the centre of a thriving artists' community but since then the artists have moved to St Ives and the town thrives as the South-West's most prominent fishing port. Newlyn is no longer pretty but parts of it are handsome, while the activity along the harbour front is all to do with the tough business of fishing, and is exciting to watch. Mousehole is still picturesque, still very much a fishing town. Its two large granite chapels are reminders of the powerful impact Wesley had on Cornwall in the eighteenth century, particularly among the impoverished miners and fisherfolk in the remote south-west, when his ideas, expressed through a compelling alchemy of declamation and ardour, revived not only the habit of worship but the identity of a religiously and mystically-inclined people. Methodism is still a force in Cornwall, and one of its legacies

White sand, turquoise sea and granite cliffs make the beauty of Porthcurno, situated on the southern shores of the Penwith peninsula.

which has reached a wider audience than Wesley might have intended is the tradition of the male-voice choirs which, with their slow and unaccompanied harmonies, bring out all that is stirring and sweet in hymns, ballads, Negro spirituals, or folk songs. Loveliest of all are the hymns Wesley wrote, and those written last century by local composers – the best known being the organist Thomas Merritt of Illogan. Many places became associated with particular hymns, and now at Christmas the carol singing in Mousehole draws people from all over Cornwall, to listen and sing. At Christmas 1981 the rejoicing was tragically muted, for less than a week before Christmas day the Penlee lifeboat had sunk with all hands lost, as well as those it had rescued. Every one of the lifeboat's crew was a Mousehole man. Even in the latter part of the twentieth century, and despite the work done by helicopter rescue teams at Culdrose and St Mawgan in North Cornwall and in other parts of Britain, we are reminded of our dependence on the sea; of its ultimate power over us; and of the heroism of those who work on it.

West Penwith is a region of granite moors ranging high across the interior to brood over the coastline. The craggy hills are dark with outcrops of granite and strewn with great boulders (for this is the land of the giants), in summer lost amid a blaze of furze, in autumn emerging from a sea of brown bracken. Perhaps more than anywhere in Cornwall the granite here records the works of man: the standing stones, logan rocks and Quoits of prehistoric ages, and the sombre outlines of engine houses from the mining boom of the eighteenth and nineteenth centuries, with chimney stacks pointing like fingers out of sweeping moorland, or staring across the rocky seas. On the south-facing shores there are no mines but the deep, steep valleys run out to coves of blue lucid water and white sands like Porthcurno, or to the National Trust's Penberth Cove which is given to fishing and growing early violets – a scatter of granite cottages and gardens sheltered by the valley slopes. Another beautiful valley, further east, is Lamorna where there are tidy cottages, a splashing river, a waterwheel and a whitewashed pub. Going further back in time, on the 'way down to Lamorna', you pass a stone circle called the Merry Maidens, and before that two standing stones known as the Pipers, Cornwall's tallest menhirs, both important Bronze-Age sites. Maidens and pipers shared the same fate as the Hurlers on Bodmin Moor.

Near Porthcurno, where present-day people dance and play in the dramatically sited open-air Minack Theatre, is the celebrated Logan (or rocking) stone, a natural phenomenon which with great effort was dislodged – and laboriously restored – by a nephew of Oliver Goldsmith, a young Lieutenant in the Royal Navy engaged in seeking out smugglers. Equally laboriously the Minack was hewn out of the granite cliff, and for 50 years it has had an active summer programme which makes this as magical a place by night as by day. An audience of another sort comes to Porthgwarra, a tiny fishing cove situated westward across the headland of Pêdn-men-an-mere, with rocky caverns and granite cottages and a valley of withies and reeds. This is a staging-post for migratory birds, and in the spring people come to watch the arrival of the whitethroats and sedge-warblers after their long journey from North Africa via the Continent to rest here before continuing to their nesting grounds throughout Britain. A path leads up the cliff to the church and church town of St Levan, romantically situated in a valley overlooking the sea. Westward along the road through St Buryan lies Land's End; or one can take the coastal path over the mossy, tufty cliffs of summer sea pinks past the towering granite promontory Tol-pedn-Penwith and its collapsed cave ceiling, which makes a great hole in the cliff, past places like Carn Lês Boel and Nanjizel, past Pardenack Point where Turner painted his stirring picture of Land's End, and all along this wild untouched coast to the most westerly point in Britain, and among the most visited.

Land's End changed ownership in 1982 and reminded the nation that it is privately owned, and can be bought and sold; more than any other wild place in Britain, people seem to take it for granted that it is theirs. Its surroundings are tawdry with *Last in England* signs, yet it can still look desolate and romantic, or at least in season a sense of scale is obtained from viewing the Land's End, one's fellow sightseers, the souvenir shops, tearoom, car park and railings from a neighbouring headland. On good days, 28 miles across the stretch of rolling water known as 'Lethosow', the Isles of Scilly are seen. A mile and a half out the Longships Lighthouse stands on its reef Carn Brâs, and eight miles out on a greenstone reef is the Wolf Rock light, whose construction seems inconceivable when south-westerly gales are blowing. An earlier, unsuccessful warning system was to have taken the form of a wolf, made of

Porthcurno's Minack Theatre, arguably Britain's most dramatically sited outdoor theatre. Theatre and creator celebrated its 50th anniversary in 1982.

copper, which would howl when gales blew through its hollow mouth: so we are told in the 1859 edition of *Murray's Handbook*. 'The violence 'of the elements,' reported Murray, 'frustrated the project.'

Man's constructions stand little chance in West Penwith unless built of the granite itself. A coastal road runs from Land's End to St Ives, and smaller roads cut across the hilly interior to the south coast of Penwith, passing many ancient sites, like the Neolithic burial chamber Lanyon Quoit, or the Iron-Age village of Chysauster high among the moors approaching the flower fields of Gulval, near Penzance. One can see the lower section, the drystone walls, of courtyard houses standing in pairs along a village way whose inhabitants, of the first century BC, would have cultivated the moors, ploughing with oxen, and streamed for tin. Their descendants of more than 2000 years have also left their mark, notably in the area around St Just-in-Penwith, near Cape Cornwall. This is an old tin-mining town, with two large and handsome Methodist chapels and a spacious church where an inscribed Celtic pillar was discovered during restoration last century. St Just, too, has an open-air theatre, a *plan-an-guare*, where Cornish Miracle Plays were performed in the Middle Ages, and where Cornish wrestling was staged. Today, the landscape around seems a veritable cemetery of defunct mines – or as the Cornish more eloquently called them, 'knackt bals' – although this district has never completely stopped working, and the old Levant mine today is incorporated into the Geevor Works at Pendeen, now working but open to visitors. The most romantic is the ruined Botallack mine where men working in levels reaching far out under the sea could hear the sound of pebbles carried by the ground-swell over their heads. The engine house stands close to the waves, the dressing sheds halfway up, and the Count House crowns the cliff face. Ironically, the boom years of 1800 to the 1860s represent a spectacular finale to an industry that was noted by Diodorus Siculus, the Greek historian of the first century BC, who commented that the tinners of Land's End (Belerion) 'are singularly fond of strangers, and, from their intercourse with foreign merchants, civilised in their habits'. By 1201, when Devon and Cornwall were granted their own Stannary Charter from King John, tin streaming and surface mining were well established. Despite the privileges granted in the Charter the medieval

tinners were among the poorest in society, although they did not share the rigours of those who worked the shaft mines during the first half of the nineteenth century. Daylight mining and streaming had been superseded by shaft mining since the fifteenth century, and as drainage techniques improved through the work of engine builders like Watt and Trevithick, shafts were sunk deeper and deeper in the quest for metal. By 1900 the Dolcoath mine, among several of similar depth, reached 470 fathoms below adit. Unless 'man engines' were used to carry the men from the surface to the levels and back, the miners descended these depths by ladder, shouldering a pick and shovel, to begin the day's picking and hewing in temperatures approaching and occasionally reaching 115°F. At the end of the day they faced the long climb back 'to grass', and a walk of perhaps five or six miles home. At peak 300 tin or copper mines were in production from Botallack to Bodmin Moor, employing 60,000 workers in or around the mines alone, producing two thirds of the world's copper. Today, farmers and townsfolk alike may still keep up family links in Australasia, Southern Africa and the Americas where at the end of the last century Cornish communities were founded as their own industry slumped through competition with newly-opening mines on all four continents.

Throughout these years the people of nearby villages like Morvah or Zennor, apart from joining the mines, continued to farm the land and fish the sea. These are granite villages in a granite land, set at the foot of craggy inland cliffs which tower up from the coast road to look across a sloping, rugged coastal plain. The seaward slopes in some places are patched with Celtic fields, divided by their stone hedges, still in use. In the small dark church of Zennor a mermaid is depicted on a bench end, comb and mirror in hand, and legend asserts that she enticed Matthew Trewhella, the churchwarden's son, to live with her beneath the waves. On the hill above Morvah, a mile or so to the south-east, is the impressive hill fort Chûn Castle of the third century BC built, unusually for that date, of stone. Like other Cornish hill castles, Chûn was reoccupied and modified during the Dark Ages, and has suffered badly in recent centuries from the plundering of builders. Further east toward Zennor, along rough footpaths and across the Penzance road, is the Mên-an-Tol holed stone, possibly of the early Bronze Age, and a ring of

The rugged granite rock formation, called by geologists 'columnar jointing', makes an appropriate Land's End at England's most westerly point.

Sunset off Land's End. On
the right is the Longships
lighthouse, occupying
the islet of Carn Brâs
about a mile offshore.
The original lighthouse,
built in 1795, was
replaced in 1883.

Blue Hills mine at Trevellas Porth, just north of St Agnes. A poignant relic of Cornwall's nineteenth century prosperity when most of the world's copper and tin came from her mines.

eleven stones, all of them invested with legends which conceal their ancient purposes. These inland cliffs are as rewarding to scramblers, hikers and climbers as they are to students of antiquities – but it should always be remembered that danger lies in mineshafts concealed beneath the undergrowth. It is hardly surprising that a wealth of legend should survive from this area, even though it is told mainly in children's story books today. Those who read of knockers, skillywiddens, spriggans, giants and mermaids must feel a shiver of recognition when they stand among these cliffs and hills. In 1870 William Botterell published his collection of droll-tellers' tales in *Traditions and Hearthside Stories of West Cornwall*, and in rewriting them hinted at links between legend and history. One series of stories, *The Giants of Towednack*, tells how young Tom killed the giant Denbras and in accordance with Denbras' wish '…before the sun sank below the hilltops, they had raised as noble a barrow over the giant, as any to be found on Towednack hills…'

Below the Towednack hills lies the ancient town of St Ives, founded by St Ia who floated across from Ireland on a leaf, or more prosaically but no less adventurously, in a coracle. The parish church occupies the site of her cell while St Ives, fishing town, artists' town, holidaymakers' and surf-riders' town, occupies the slopes on either side of a headland called the Island which juts westward into St Ives Bay. When the railway arrived the old town was attracting the active and distinguished artists' colony which later laid a restraining hand on development, and helped preserve St Ives' charm. The industries that created that charm, the pilchard fisheries that built the fish cellars and the mining industry that sent ore from the port, have faded. By the 'boom years' of the nineteenth century pilchard fishing had changed little in principle from the thirteenth century, when supplies of salt from France first permitted preservation. Only in the present century have we seen the dispersal of the shoals through climatic changes and overfishing. The fish were taken by drifting – stretching nets offshore and relying on the fish to get caught in the mesh – or by seining, the more dramatic

method, where entire shoals were captured in nets according to the directions of the clifftop huer 'crying with a loud voice', according to Carew, 'whistling through his fingers, and wheazing certain diversified and significant signs with a bush which he holdeth in his hand'. In any of the peak years of the eighteenth or nineteenth centuries more than 300 seine boats might employ almost 3000 people at sea and more than 6000 might be engaged in the fish cellars. The fish, pressed, salted and packed in hogsheads, were exported to Italy from the four main ports, St Ives, Penzance, Falmouth and Fowey. The wry humour of the Cornish is expressed in a well-known toast of the time, 'Long life to the Pope, death to our best friends, and may our streets run in blood.'

The last seine-fishing in St Ives was seen in 1924, and finally it was the deep-sea trawling industry which broke up the shoals, not only of pilchard but of mackerel and herring, and destroyed the immature fish. The same confrontation takes place today, although St Ives like other Cornish ports has its quota of fishing craft – but the days are gone when Hamilton

Jenkin in the 1920s could write of the 'fall of a winter's afternoon' at St Ives, watching 'the herring fleet as it goes streaking out across the darkening waters of the bay.'

So too might the St Ives painters, sculptors, potters, printers, illustrators have watched the same fleets. Artists' names best-known outside St Ives are Barbara Hepworth and Ben Nicholson, and their work is exhibited locally – particularly the work of Barbara Hepworth, at her former home and at the Barbara Hepworth Museum and Sculpture Gardens in Back Street, and in the church of St Ia, where her Madonna and Child is seen in the Lady Chapel. Coming into the town from Zennor, passing through Stennack, you can visit the potter Bernard Leach's studio before taking the winding streets to the waterfront.

West Penwith, Cornwall's Cornwall, should not be left without a climb to the top of Trencrom Hill, to look across the moors to both coasts of Cornwall: St Michael's Mount in its distant shining bay; Godrevy lighthouse far across St Ives Bay where the Red River carries its rust-red ore from Carnmenellis Moors to the sea.

Beach-huts, palms and sea at Portminster Beach, St Ives. Formerly one of Cornwall's chief pilchard fishing ports, St Ives today is a mecca for holidaymakers and artists.

4 Atlantic Grandeur

The high land around St Ives looks north-west past the Hayle Estuary and Godrevy Point along the Atlantic coastline – the 'north coast' which for many people conjures ideas of majestic headlands, golf courses, sand and surf. The stretch between Godrevy and Newquay has some but not all of these things, and again the age of tin mining is recalled by engine houses abandoned in lonely cliff valleys swamped in bracken or gorse. The scene is set at Godrevy Head where the Red River rushes down across the sand to colour St Ives Bay a muddy red. Godrevy lighthouse gleaming white against the green turf, red breakers and blue horizon looks as if it is here for visual effect, but the seas are no less treacherous along these shores. The grassy dunes of Upton Downs give way at Godrevy to high stern cliffs where seals breed in caves accessible only from the sea. The roadside spectacle, 'Hell's Mouth,' when restless dark water at high tide pounds the rocks below, seems hellish indeed. At Portreath, seaside bungalows and surf riders are a late twentieth-century additon to this old mining port.

Mining nourished the growth of Hayle, Camborne and Redruth whose chapels, town halls, railways and viaducts owe much in stonework and cast iron to Victorian mining technology. Cornish porches of white-painted wood or iron enriched with coloured glass, and dark cypresses or firs or even palms, add colour to these granite towns. Lord Dunstanville who built Portreath's docks and railway is commemorated by a spiky beacon crowning Carn Brea which with its prehistoric fort looms over the landscape but gives stupendous views towards two coasts across the moors with their mine workings and smoky towns. On the road between Camborne and Redruth the National Trust preserves a beam engine of the 1870s, used for winding men and ore from a depth of nearly 1500 feet, and other pumping engines can be seen at Taylor's shaft in Camborne's East Pool mine, or at the recently reopened South Crofty mine. In Camborne itself outside the public library is the statue of the great engineer Richard Trevithick, who developed the beam engine and invented a steam locomotive that would carry passengers. On its historic trial run the locomotive was parked half-way up Beacon Hill in a stable while Trevithick and his elated party repaired to an inn, whereupon a spark from the 'puffing devil' set light to the stable roof. The incident is remembered by Cornishmen and rugby players in the song 'Camborne Hill,' but the living legacy of Trevithick and of other pioneering Camborne engineers is the town's School of Metalliferous Mining, known throughout the world. East of Redruth, carved into the slopes of Carn Marth, is a turf-covered arena known as Gwennap Pit where the aged John Wesley preached to thousands and afterwards wrote in his *Journal*, 'this is my *ne plus ultra*. I shall scarce see a larger congregation till we meet in the air.' Across to the north, close by the sea, St Agnes Beacon rises 629 feet above the town sheltering on its slopes. St Agnes, the last of the coastal mining towns, is the birthplace of the painter John Opie who rose to fashionable fame in London and was buried in the crypt of St Paul's Cathedral. A steep valley leads from his town to Trevaunance Cove, where attempts to build a small port failed because the sea washed the walls and pier away.

The parish of Perranzubaloe, near St Agnes, has strong associations with St Piran who is

the patron saint of tin miners, and some would say of Cornwall. Nearly two miles east of Perranporth, now a typical north Cornish resort, is the old *plân-an-guare* Piran Round where recently the Cornish Miracle Plays have been revived. In the long stretch of coastal duneland between Perranporth and Ligger Point is the lost church of St Piran, a pre-Conquest building abandoned in the eleventh century, suffocated by drifting sand and rediscovered in 1800, but now reburied for its own preservation. The sand dunes themselves are protected by belonging to the Ministry of Defence preventing the private or speculative building which even in these enlightened times rarely manages to construct anything which does not mar the beauties of the landscape. North of Ligger Head, the coast becomes benevolent. Dunes face out across the sands of Holywell Bay, the turf-topped cliffs of Kelsey Head and Pentire Point hold the enchanting cove of Porth Joke, and low water in the Gannel estuary reveals acres of sand. A mile or so east of Ligger Point, the small spire of Cubert is prominent in all this treeless, windy land, and less than a mile east the Newquay road carries holiday traffic in search of sand and surf.

Newquay is Cornwall's biggest and brashest holiday resort and has developed in layers of hotels, guest houses and bungalows around the old harbour and essentially Cornish main street. By the quayside are the oldest buildings and even some of the original pilot gigs that used to race for the job of guiding in cargo boats. They still race every week in the summer, when wind and weather allow, but these races are solely for sport. Up on the Headland the whitewashed stone huer's hut watches harbour and sea, as it has since the prosperous days before the pilchard shoals failed and before the railway arrived in 1875 bringing not minerals, as had been intended, but visitors. Trenance Gardens were laid out early this century with their ordered paths, shrubs and boating lake, a golf-course occupies the dunes of Fistral Beach, and recently the town has opened an excellent zoo. The unfailing attraction is the golden sand of Tolcarne and Towan beaches,

Perran Sands: the cult sport of the 'sixties, Malibu board riding still provides a way of life for some, and for many others a thrilling holiday pastime.

Newquay Harbour. Original pilot gigs still race every week in the summer season from Cornwall's biggest and brashest holiday resort.

whether felt between the toes or viewed from the high headland walks or from the great hotels which defy winter gales for the sake of a panorama on the grand scale: wide, glistening beaches at the foot of huge cliffs reaching right up the coast to Trevose Head, all subjected to the long Atlantic swell. Since the '60s Newquay has attracted a colony of surfers, looking like medieval knights in their wetsuits, who have dared the rollers in a way no local fisherman would ever think of doing. As Cornish male voice choirs put it in the *Newquay Fisherman's Song*:

Sometimes the waves rise high, and wild winds roar;
The angry breakers roll along the rocky shore;
Tis then for cosy home we haul, and dear ones waiting
    there –
And trust our lives to One above, Who listens to our
    prayer.

Between Newquay and Bedruthan a coast road rides the clifftop plateaux and the valleys between. Out of season on a fine day the sudden views of headlands, serried breakers and golden sands make this one of the most exciting drives in the Duchy, with stretches of beach that rival

anything California has to offer. At Mawgan Porth a road leading inland along the Vale of Lanherne shows how unspoiled the rural countryside remains, although such narrow roads, and massive Cornish hedges, make no concession for summer motorists. The Vale shelters one of North Cornwall's loveliest villages, St Mawgan in Pydar, its houses scattered about the hillsides and around a bridge over a plashing stream, canopied by the tall trees of the Carnanton woods. The fifteenth-century church stands beside a

Cliff scenery at its finest at Bedruthan. Low tide reveals a vast expanse of rock, sand and deep rock-pools overlooked by the turf-covered heights.

Carmelite nunnery whose manor house was a gift of the powerful Arundel family in 1794. It is hard to believe such a peaceful and sheltered place could exist so close to the Atlantic until you walk in these woods, or stand in the mossy churchyard at St Columb Major which overlooks the head of the Vale, or climb the magnificent hill of Castle-an-Dinas, a three-ringed hill fort on the St Austell road, where the calm of the inland countryside prevails. It is in these out-of-the-way places, too, that old customs linger – the St Columb hurling game is still played, once on Shrove Tuesday and then the following Saturday, using a silvered ball with the inscription *Guare wheag yu guare teag*: 'Gentle play is handsome play.' From Castle-an-Dinas, on Midsummer Eve, can be seen the blaze of beacon fires that are lit on all the old, high hills of Cornwall – Carn Brea, Tregonning, Trencrom – an ancient custom that had died out, but was revived by the Old Cornwall Society in 1929, while it was still alive in old people's memories.

A demonstration of the power of the sea, which wrecked the *Good Samaritan* at Bedruthan in 1850, is remembered in the rhyme:

> The *Good Samaritan* came ashore
> To feed the hungry and clothe the poor,
> Barrels of beef and bales of linen,
> No poor man shall want of a shillin'.

Bedruthan is a nationally-known beauty spot famous for its clifftop view over a vast expanse of sands with great rocks flung as if by a giant. The Queen Bess Rock, so-called because it resembled Queen Elizabeth I, was a well-known feature until in 1981 the unfortunate lady lost her head in a storm. The sands, caverns, pools and mussel-covered rocks have been accessible at times by steps cut into the cliff face, but these are perilous and the National Trust, whose land this is, has at times closed access. In fact this and other beaches nearby are dangerous to bathe from because in all weathers undercurrents are powerful enough to drag even good swimmers away, and safety warnings should always be heeded. From Bedruthan can be seen the tower of the parish church, St Eval, which has served as a landmark since it fell in 1727 and was re-built by Bristol merchants for their captains making their way along these dangerous shores. Many of the local names for the deep dark coves recall bounty that they have provided – Wine Cove, Butter Cove, Pepper Cove. Periodically after gales at sea smooth black stones washed up on the sands can be used for coal, which is what they are. The

collier which provided this cheap fuel went down off the coast more than 60 years ago. Modern deck cargo, spars and hatch covers are still gratefully claimed and used in patching fences on the small farms that occupy the plateau lands and valleys, independent of coastal caravans, bungalows, and golf-courses.

From here to Padstow extends a sequence of wild clifflands and sandy bays, excellent for careful surfing. The wildness is softened by the springiness of the turf and the cliff flowers of summer, or the domestic touch of hedges and fields in winter. In the gardens, sheltered by high hedges of evergreen, Fuchsia and Escallonia grow, while sea holly and sea spinach flourish among the sand dunes. Near Padstow Trevose Head lighthouse, set on a windy headland, is approached by high-hedged lanes and a toll road. Further along the coast past Mother Ivey's Bay at Cataclews Point is the slate quarry which has been worked since medieval times and originally was named *Carrack-looze*, meaning 'Grey-blue rock'. Its popularity in those days derived from its durability, and also from its fine grain which made it suitable for carving. The quarry's parish church at St Merryn has a very beautiful font of catacleuse stone, taken from the sand-locked church of Constantine whose ruins can be seen on Constantine golf course. Past the quarries at Harlyn Bay an Iron-Age cemetery found earlier this century yielded bones and artefacts, among them the skeleton of a child apparently buried with two mice. We cannot tell whether the mice were pets, symbols or sacrifices for we can only guess at what the birds and beasts meant to these Iron-Age tribesmen. The earliest Cornish legends probably date from this age in which the Cornish race itself has its origins. A later legend tells of the transmigration of King Arthur's soul into a Cornish chough, the national bird, a graceful scarlet-beaked crow of the wild sea-cliffs. It is now a decade since the last chough in Cornwall died somewhere along this coast, but the Arthurian legend still attracts visitors to Tintagel and other legendary sites.

The old town of Padstow is gathered around its harbour which looks eastward to the sands of Rock across the Camel estuary, where a ferry has operated since the days of the Black Prince, who was first lessor. Behind the harbour the streets amble this way and that, mostly uphill. North of the harbour mouth a path leads to Chapel Stile, past St George's Well and out along the northern cliffs which stretch to distant Stepper Point, and

the open sea. On the harbour's North Quay stands the fifteenth-century Guildhall, now known as Abbey House, and on South Quay is Raleigh's Courthouse where he presided when he was Warden of Cornwall. Padstow has been an important place at least since the sixth century, when St Petroc arrived from Wales with 60 disciples, and founded a monastery here. Until Saxon domination, or perhaps until the Danes ravaged the town in 981, Padstow remained the ecclesiastical centre of Cornwall and thereafter it was prominent as a fishing and boat-building town, and as a port. Even after the harbour silted up in the last century, Padstow's industries were able to continue on a local scale because the railway provided a link with the major routes up-river. Spreading inland from the harbour the town climbs the steep wooded cliffs which rise in a protective semi-circle. Under the trees is the church of St Petroc with its original barrel roof, elaborate and beautiful catacleuse font, bench-end carving of a fox preaching to geese, and fine Prideaux family tombs. The wooded cliffs curve round from the Victorian Hotel Metropole to Prideaux Place in its deer park, the manor house with castellated façade and mullioned windows that has been occupied by the Prideaux family since the Reformation, when it was built. Here on May morning, for Padstow's traditional May Day celebrations, the 'Obby 'Oss and Teaser come to perform their complex and grotesque ritual dance of the death and resurrection of summer in homage to the family assembled on the lawn. To the Maysong chanted by the followers, accompanied by the band and pagan drum, the dancers thread through the town all day accompanied by folk singing pilgrims from all over Britain.

Only in the last 15 years with the closing of the railway has Padstow become too isolated for local trade and abandoned itself to tourism, leaving business to workaday Wadebridge whose bridge, at the lowest crossing of the Camel, was 'the longest, strongest and fairest that the shire can muster,' according to Carew, and carried 17 arches on powerful piers of local stone. Its building in the sixteenth century was said to have included woolpacks for foundations, but whether physically, or fiscally, is not known. Padstow has become a town of shellshops and souvenirs but the local people remain the same, Padstonian to the core, rightly proud of their lifeboat, still in awe of the dangerous Doom Bar and the other sandbars which underlie the blue waters stretching across to the golden sands

of Rock. On Christmas Eve the townspeople crowd into the hall at Prideaux Place, where the family listen to the harmonies of the Padstow Carols sung unaccompanied – words and melodies known only in this town.

It is said that St Petroc first landed at Trebetherick and astonished harvesters in the fields by striking a rock with his staff to produce a gush of water, after which he astonished them even more by crossing the estuary, with no local guide, to arrive safely at what is now Hawker's Cove just north of Padstow. Since the age of the 'seaside', visitors have arrived at this stretch of estuary coast between Trebetherick Point and Rock, and stayed – to enjoy Rock's sand dunes, the golf course, and the sands at Daymer Bay overlooked by grassy Brea Hill. Hard by the golf course is the Norman chapel-of-ease St Enodoc, once so inundated by sand that the parson and his flock were obliged to enter through a hole in the roof. Since then the sands have been planted with marram grass, and the small cruciform chapel with its thirteenth-century tower and spire, hedged about with tamarisk and carefully restored, has resisted the fate of other sand-bound churches. On summery days these parts show North Cornwall at its softest – old buildings of slate, drifting pale sands, silvery 'spires' bent and shimmering with wind, wisps of tamarisk all greyish-green, and on some days the sea at rest: silent, hazy, powder-blue. Sir John Betjeman's well-known poem recalls a different aspect:

> But when the storm was at its height
> And feathery slate was black with rain,
> And tamarisks were hung with light
> And golden sand was brown again,
> Spring and blizzard would unite
> And sea come flooding up the lane.

Ocean storms power the long rollers which are ideal for surfing, and provide one of the joys of Polzeath; built-up and no longer beautiful, it is among Cornwall's finest surfing beaches. Here the shoreline protrudes northward beyond the shelter of the estuary and Pentire Point juts out, with the Rumps, to give incomparable cliff views as far north as Hartland Point, and lovely walking country for the next seven miles or so to Port Isaac over land that is largely owned by the National Trust. This is North Cornwall as our grandparents must have found it – coastal farms and fields reaching toward the cliff edge, sandy coves for bathing held between rugged but not unfriendly cliffs, the soft turf full of small flowers and fat cushions of sea-pink in early summer

The ruins of Tintagel Castle, built to confirm Norman supremacy just over 100 years after Cornwall's subjugation by Saxon England.

The Old Post Office near
Tintagel, one of the finest
examples of a small
medieval manor house
in Britain.

The entrance to Boscastle Harbour, awe-inspiring and difficult, the only haven along miles of treacherous north Cornish and Devonshire coastline.

when the gulls, oyster catchers and shags are at their noisiest. High on the inland plateau stands the church of St Endellion, dedicated to St Endelienta, isolated but for the rectory and prebendal houses. This is the simple but exquisite setting for music festivals which are important events in Cornwall's seasonal diary. Here, and at St Columb, festivals grew from a series of chamber and choral concerts that were given one summer by music students who spent the previous week in rehearsals in this lovely setting, and shared the proceeds of the concert with the church. Now fully-qualified musicians, the former students and the accompanying choir have continued the tradition. One pleasant product of the festival has been the formation of the professional chamber group the St Endellion Quartet, which has carried the name of this saint that lived only on cow's milk – the eldest of King Brychan's saintly daughters – far beyond her adopted Cornwall.

Until 1913 St Endellion was the parish church for Port Isaac, reached along two miles of road that descends in a series of loops and turns to the slate-hung cottages of the fishing port, built on steep slopes either side of the sandy harbour. The open fields in view above the town, the tiny lanes with the stream splashing between, and the lack of car parks keep the character and beauty of the place intact, while the two Methodist chapels and Victorian schoolhouse point to its former importance as a fishing and corn port. A mile or so towards Polzeath, another road twists and turns down a pretty valley past ivy-covered ruins of cottages to a narrow inlet at the head of which Portquin's fish cellars now serve as holiday accommodation, and three waterside holiday cottages are maintained by the National Trust. The hamlet was said to have been abandoned after its fishermen went out one day and failed to return. The tragedy was the subject of the best-known painting to come out of the Newlyn School – Frank Bramley's *A Hopeless Dawn*. However in the *Penguin Guide* of 1939 the author notes that Portquin was 'called "decayed" in 1584, and has remained so.' The Trust has kept the approach road rough, making this a peaceful seaside place for people prepared to risk their car springs, or to walk.

North of Port Isaac the coast becomes even more unapproachable and as far as Trebarwith Strand, for about five miles, no road reaches it. Streams rise on high ground a mile or so inland and rush through overgrown valleys to the cliffs,

scarred with slate workings. Two miles inland of Tregardock the famous Delabole slate quarry is experiencing its first dramatic fall in demand – through the introduction of cheap but good imitation roofing slates – since Tudor times. The quarries continue to work, however, and stoneworking skills can be watched from observation platforms forming part of a working museum. Trebarwith Strand with its long sands and great caverns, now a favoured seaside spot, once had slate workings and handled the export of stone from Delabole through the hamlet of Treknow. A little way north, at gloomy Dunderhole Head, the quarry buildings house a youth hostel. The idea of working these cliffs

in fine weather when the water sparkles and the rock is hot – thankless work though it may have been – seems very different from the harsh image conjured by wet black slate, angry seas, and finger-numbing wind and rain.

At Tintagel the realities of working the cliff face are forgotten, and the ancient myth of Arthur takes hold, even on the approach down slatey lanes with tantalising glimpses of the sea. In response to the popularity of the castle a village has grown, and is situated about a quarter of a mile from the site. An incongruous survivor in this strip of souvenir shops is a medieval manor house of great interest and charm. It is called the Old Post Office, from the purpose it served in Victoria's day. Built in the fourteenth century, it is one of the oldest hall houses in Britain, and one of the few modest dwellings of this period that can be visited. The National Trust maintains one of the rooms as a Victorian village post office. The castle itself in its awesome setting fulfils all expectations. Its ruins occupy both sides of a high and narrow causeway across which a dizzying bridge leads to the 'island,' which has the remains of a fifth-century monastery on its summit. On wild days the scene is at its most terrifying but even on still summer days the drama is strong. It is here, so legend says, that with the assistance of Merlin's magic Uther Pendragon visited Queen Igraine in the guise of her husband Gorlois, King of Cornwall. Pendragon eventually overcame Gorlois in battle and became King of Cornwall and on his death Arthur, son of Pendragon and Igraine, succeeded his father as King. The legend has been traced to Geoffrey of Monmouth writing in the twelfth century and to Sir Thomas Malory of the fifteenth century, and has been taken up by Carew and used by Tennyson: this century, Arthur's associations with Tintagel have been dismissed as nonsense. It is warming to find the respected Charles Henderson writing in 1928,

In the writer's opinion this criticism is excessive. The recent discovery of 5th-6th century graves on the Castle Island, the presence of two Roman milestones in the parish, one found in the churchyard, the other at Trethevy, and the existence of a little chapel on the Island dedicated to the Celtic Julitta, all incline him to think that Tintagel was a place of capital importance at the very period when Arthur was flourishing.

The castle was begun early in the thirteenth century, possibly on the site of a manor house, but the fabric that remains dates from the ownership of Henry III's younger brother Richard. The Celtic monastery seems to have been abandoned within a century of the castle's establishment, a move which may have resulted from Norman occupation of the island. In the twelfth century the Normans built the church which is dedicated to St Materiana, and which stands apart on a bleak cliff south of the island and castle. The church is still used, and in the churchyard headstones have to be shored up against the wind. The Elizabethan vicarage is occupied, although its slate pigeon house is empty. The castle, and the earlier habitations on the island, are occupied by the spirit of Cornwall's Celtic past.

Boscastle and its surroundings are possibly more dramatic but here the natural, rather than the supernatural, dominates. And even as Cornwall draws towards its border we see, perhaps to greater effect than anywhere, that unmistakably Cornish fusion of water and foliage and stone. The harbour itself is extraordinary, a natural inlet that affords the only shelter on all this merciless coast from Padstow beyond Hartland Point to Appledore. Even then it makes a terrifying entrance along a narrow twisting channel between sprawling cliffs, with the harbour constructed at the point where a confluence of two rushing streams meets the tide. The old town climbs up from the remains of a Norman castle built where the wooded Valency and Jordan valleys meet. The harbour divides two parishes, and the town's nearest church Forrabury is built above the grassy cliffs beside Forrabury Common, to the west of the harbour, where the Celtic system of 'stitchmeal' field tenure survives. Forrabury church suffered drastic restoration in the last century but a mile or so to the north, on a wooded slope above the Valency, Thomas Hardy as a young architect restored the church of St Juliot, with kinder results. Perhaps his thoughtful treatment resulted from his meeting Emma Gifford here, and from the spectacular river and cliff scenery of their courtship which formed the setting for Hardy's novel *A Pair of Blue Eyes*.

From Boscastle the cliffs range higher and grimmer, with welcome gaps at Crackington Haven and Widemouth Bay, and Bude. Inland are the valleys and lanes, the streams, the old farms, the grey churches in their wind-pruned trees. Gorse and heather and bracken cover the cliff valleys. The Atlantic slaps and lashes at the contorted rocks of this coastline or it lies quiet, so that the immensity of its waters can be seen beneath their gentle swell. This country where the peregrine falcon roams, so close to the Devon border, is as far off the beaten track as the wild places of the moor, the sequestered southern estuaries or the far country of giants and mermaids around the Land's End. Across the Tamar, the Celtic *Great Water*, another world begins.